SOCIAL EMOTIONAL LEARNING
Guide for Positive Thinking

RED, YELLOW & GREEN FEELINGS

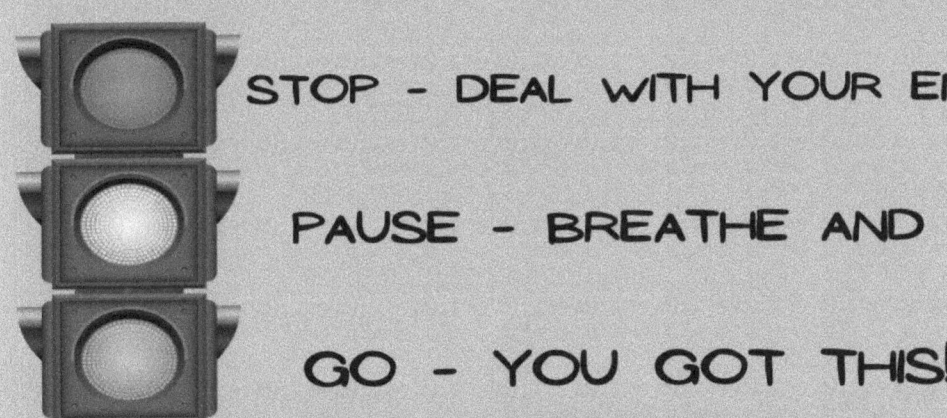

STOP - DEAL WITH YOUR EMOTIONS

PAUSE - BREATHE AND RELAX

GO - YOU GOT THIS!

Tips to Handle Anxiety, Stress and Other Emotions

For ages 8+

Kim Roshone

Disclaimer

This workbook is intended for informational purposes only and is not a substitute for professional mental health advice, diagnosis, or treatment. The activities and exercises provided are general in nature and should not be considered a replacement for personalized care from a licensed mental health professional. If you are experiencing mental health concerns or crises, we strongly encourage you to seek the support of a qualified therapist, counselor, or healthcare provider. The creator of this workbook is not responsible for any outcomes resulting from the use of the information contained herein. Always consult with a healthcare professional before making any decisions regarding your mental health and well-being.

Copyright © 2025 by Kim Roshone.

All rights reserved. No portion of this book may be reproduced, stored in a retrieval system, or transmitted by any form or any means electronically, photocopied, recorded, or any other except for brief quotations in printed reviews, without the prior permission of the publisher.

Cover design by Senir Design. Contact info: info@senirdesign.com

ISBN # 979-8-9925784-1-6

TABLE OF CONTENTS

Overview	9
A Note to Caregivers and Educators	10
A Note to Youth and Teens	11
Instructions for Using Workbook	12
About Me	13
Feelings	14
Feelings Wheel	15
Feelings in Your Body	16
Section 1 – Red Light Topics	17
Anger	19
Anxiety	20
Bullied	21
Depressed	22
Disappointed	23
Embarrassed	24
Fear	25
Grief	26
Guilt	27
Irritated	28
Jealous	29
Lonely	30
Pressured	31
Sadness	32
Scared	33
Stressed	34
Worried	35
Worrying and Triggers	36
Tracking the Triggers	37
Final Thoughts on Section 1	38
Section 2 – Yellow Light Topics	39
Affirmations	41

Alphabet	42
Blowing Bubbles to Stay Calm	43
Breathing Exercises 1	44
Breathing Exercises 2	45
Color the Butterflies	46
Coloring Your Way to Calmness	47
Countdown by 5	48
Counting Backwards	49
Create a Poem, Song or Rap	50
Create a Story	51
Create a Story Using the 5 Senses	52
Creative Thinking	53
Daily Gratitude	54
Daily Reflection	55
Exercise Time	56
Grounding Techniques	57
I Am Affirmations	58
Journal Activity	59
Journal Writing	60
Mental Health Check	61
Mental Health Check In	62
Mindfulness	63
Positive Word List	64
Relaxation Word Search	65
Things I Like	66
Trace the Patterns	67
Trace the Patterns (Part 2)	68
Visualization	69
More About Feelings	70
More About Me	71

Section 3 – Green Light Topics   73

Character	75
Confidence	76
Discovering Differences	77

Emotional Regulation	78
Finding Joy	79
Goal Setting	80
Gratitude	81
Happiness	82
Identity	83
Kindness	84
Love Who I Am	85
Mental Health	86
Mindset	87
Positive Thinking and Positive Self-Talk	88
Purpose	89
Reflection	90
Relationship Skills	91
Responsible Decision-Making	92
Self-Awareness	93
Self-Esteem	94
Self-Management	95
Social Awareness	96
Teamwork	97
Time Management	98

Section 4 – Construction Zone — 99

Wellness Toolkit	101
Self-Esteem Jar	102
Confidence Collage	103
Action Plan	104
My Goals	105
Draw a Picture	106
Work in Progress	107
Express Yourself	108
Do Something Fun	109
Celebrate Me	110
Notes Page	111
Answers to Word Search	112

Final Project	113
Conclusion	**115**
Bibliography	**116**
Acknowledgements & About the Author	**117**

Overview of RED, YELLOW & GREEN FEELINGS

Red, Yellow & Green Feelings was created to assist students in understanding and expressing their feelings, in learning coping strategies, in developing empathy, in forming relationships, in building confidence and in increasing self-esteem. The way we think and behave affects our well-being and mental health. Challenges are going to happen in life, and as we deal with them, instead of avoiding them, we begin to change our thought patterns. As children learn to deal with their emotions, they become better at problem solving and increasing their self-confidence.

Think of a red light on the street. The red light means we must stop. Our emotions can feel overwhelming at times, and we need to stop and process what is happening. The first section of this workbook covers the various negative feelings and emotions we experience in life and provides tips for identifying triggers. This section covers a variety of topics children face, such as stress, fear, and worrying, which can affect their learning and development.

Think of a yellow light. The yellow light means we need to pause or slow down. When our emotions try to take over, we need to pause, take a deep breath, and remain calm. This section of the workbook has instructions on how to achieve this. A variety of coping strategies, such as breathing techniques, mindfulness activities and positive self-talk, will be featured in this section.

Now, think of a green light. The green light means GO! A person can go and be whoever he/she wants to be. People have the power to be whoever they set their mind and heart on. It's important to have a positive mindset to deal with the many challenges we face in life. This third section will include tips and strategies to build confidence and boost self-esteem.

The fourth and final section focuses on creating a plan to feel empowered and resilient. Learning healthy ways to deal with negative emotions can help children short-term and on their journey in becoming a successful adult. Goals, an action plan, and journaling are all great examples for reflection. The reader will have an opportunity to think in depth about what they learned and what they plan to do next for success.

Note to Caregivers and Educators

Greetings!

I am so thrilled to share this workbook with a special person in your care. We draw children in with love and kindness, and we show we care by genuine concern for their well-being. *Red, Yellow & Green Feelings* is a curriculum designed to support your work because I respect you, value your expertise, and your desire in wanting the best for your child or student.

Life is filled with so many challenges, and our emotions can be overwhelming. This workbook will cover topics, such as anxiety, anger, depression, along with tips to deal with these feelings. Social emotional learning focuses on developing emotional intelligence, self-awareness, and interpersonal skills. This can help students manage their emotions, build healthy relationships, and reduce unwanted behavior.

When a child does not have an opportunity to process, give meaning, and learn to cope with a traumatic experience with a trusted adult, the trauma can have a devastating impact at the time and on subsequent development. Trauma can affect learning, behavior, and school performance. Students need guidance and support with identity development, cognitive processing, behavior management, moral development, and the ability to trust themselves and others. We want our children to make good decisions and develop meaningful relationships with others. Children need to learn to separate their feelings from who they are as a person.

I welcome and encourage you to talk to your child or student about what he/she is going through, what he/she is learning, and ask if he/she needs any support or guidance. Many people, including adults, do not feel comfortable sharing their feelings with anyone, and their feelings should be embraced. Mental health is an essential component of overall health and well-being. It enables us to experience joy, build resilience, and maintain a sense of purpose.

I hope this workbook with inspire and help someone to manage his/her emotions, cope with challenges, maintain great relationships, and lead a productive life.

Note to Youth and Teens

Hello,

This workbook is to help you on your journey. I am hopeful that you will be more in tune with your feelings, thoughts, and behaviors, and work through them while making good choices.

Dealing with emotions is an important skill to learn, and learning coping strategies, such as breathing exercises and practicing mindfulness, can help. Learning healthy ways to handle frustration, stress, and worry will help both short-term and hopefully long-term as an adult.

I work with students who need assistance with their feelings and emotions. I want to offer tips and suggestions to help you manage your emotions and use strategies to stay calm and be successful. Most importantly, I want to provide guidance about what has helped my students feel better about themselves and thrive. I want the best for you as well.

Let's get started!

Instructions for using this workbook:

Talking about our feelings helps us feel better. You will learn more and more about your feelings, thoughts, and behaviors, which is important. The first section of the workbook is designed to help you work through the feelings and emotions you may go through. Each topic is explained, and you can share your experience, if any, that applies to you.

The second section is designed to teach you a variety of coping strategies to stay calm, to be relaxed, to think before reacting, and distraction activities. The more you practice these strategies, the easier it will be for you to apply these methods when things happen.

The third section of the workbook is designed to help you build confidence in yourself, have meaningful relationships with your peers and adults, and provide opportunities to practice positive self-talk. The goal is to turn negative thoughts into positive thoughts as much as possible.

The fourth section includes activities for you to build the life you want. You will produce an action plan, list your special qualities, and create a final project. You should use this section to remind yourself of how great you are, especially when you're not feeling your best.

About Me

Feelings

How are you feeling today?

Angry	Happy	Embarrassed
Guilt	Scared	Sad
Calm	Worried	Confident
Excited	Proud	Irritable

Feelings Wheel

Look at the many feelings on the emotional wheel.

List any of these feelings or emotions you have felt:

Feelings in Your Body

Whenever we experience negative emotions, our body can show a variety of physical signs.

Here is a list of some of the reactions:

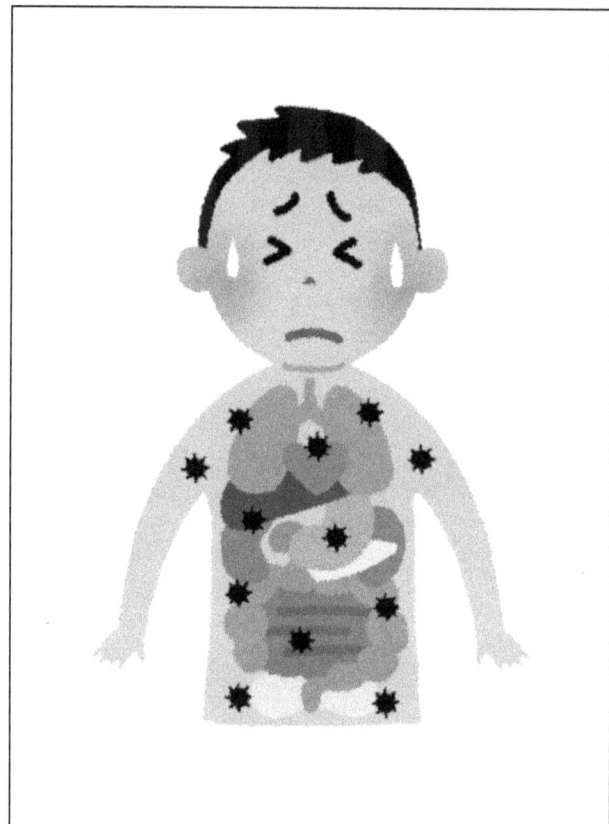

Fast heartbeat
Sweating
Dizziness
Teary eyes
Headache
Stomachache
Tense muscles
Fast breathing
Shaking
Blushing

Remember, you are not alone. We all experience physical signs in the body. You will get through this. Be brave, and remember to just breathe.

Section 1

Anger

It is normal to feel angry. It's about how you handle the feeling. When people get mad or angry, they might yell, hold the feelings inside, or throw something. Anger is a natural, often intense, emotional response to frustrations, threats, or perhaps injustices. Anger that is not handled properly or addressed can lead to anxiety, depression, or stress.

Pay attention to situations that cause anger and try to avoid them if possible. If you can't avoid them, try to stay calm and practice deep breathing.

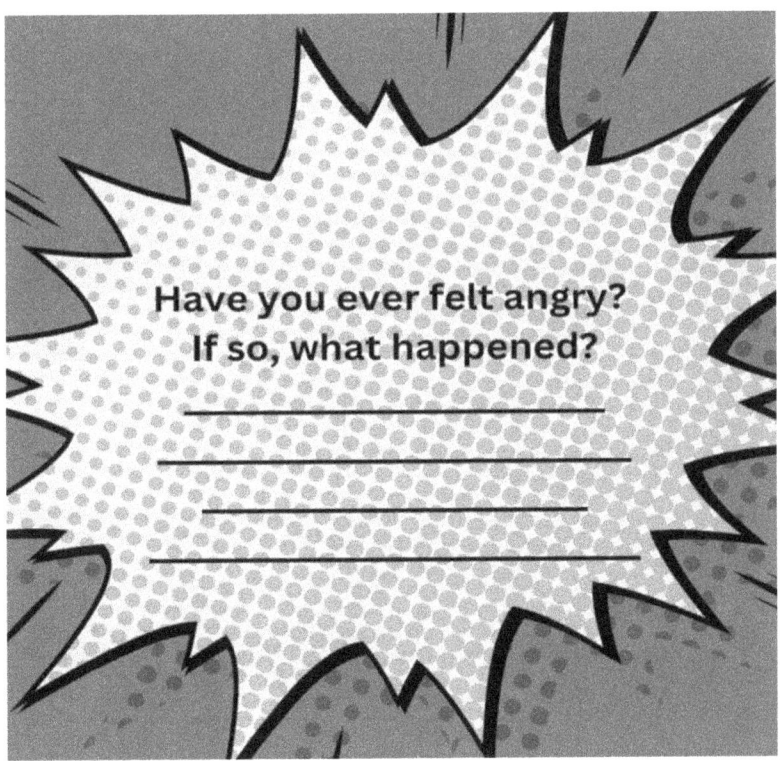

Tip - A great way to deal with anger is to begin deep breathing and remember to think carefully before saying something you may regret. You can count down from 99 to 1. As you count down, take deep breaths...inhale and exhale. Repeat as many times as needed.

Anxiety

Anxiety or feeling anxious is a feeling of fear and uneasiness. Being anxious may interfere with your ability to function. You may have feelings of panic and difficulty concentrating. Sometimes, stress can make a person feel anxious. A person may feel nervous and unable to stay calm when he/she is feeling anxious. Some physical symptoms could include a fast-beating heart, shortness of breath, sweating, and tense muscles or tiredness.

Have you ever felt anxious about something? What happened, and what did you do to feel better?

A great way to deal with anxiety is to think of something that is calming. Visualization is a great strategy to use where you can picture yourself at a happy place. A happy place can be at the beach, the mountains, or playing in the snow.

Name your happy place: _____

Remember, if you ever feel anxious, think of your happy place.

Bullied

Feeling bullied is when someone has been threatened or teased. This behavior is often repeated and shows an imbalance of power. Bullying can be mental, verbal, or physical. Bullying can also include spreading rumors and excluding someone from a group on purpose. Another form of bullying is cyberbullying, which is the use of technology to harass, threaten, or embarrass someone. If bullying happens, report it to an adult. If someone is cyberbullying, do not respond and save the evidence. Talk to a teacher, counselor, or family member, so you can get support and develop a plan to stop the bullying.

Has someone ever bullied you? If so, how did you feel, and did you report it to someone?

Tips on bullying
- Take deep breaths, speak calmly, and show confidence.
- Write down what happened in case you need to report the incident to the authorities or in seeking help.
- Remember, it's not your fault, and sometimes, bullies act out because of their own pain.
- Write in a journal to express your feelings.

Depressed

Depression is when you have feelings of sadness, hopelessness, and a loss of interest in activities you once enjoyed. Depression can affect how a person thinks, feels, and behaves. Feeling depressed can sometimes last for days, weeks, or months. A person may have difficulty focusing and thinking clearly. If an individual feels depressed, he/she should try and build strong relationships with family and friends. When depressed, a person may feel sadness and have difficulty focusing and making decisions. Remember to speak to a counselor if you need help.

Have you ever felt depressed about something? If you feel comfortable, share what made you feel this way.

\
\
\
\
\
\

There is help with depression with lifestyle changes, support, and sometimes therapy. Talk to a counselor or trusted adult, and whenever possible, eat healthy foods, exercise, relax, and remember to breathe. Think positively, draw, keep a gratitude journal, and most importantly, treat yourself with kindness.

Disappointed

Disappointment is a feeling when your hopes, desires, or expectations are not met. Feeling disappointed can lead to feelings of sadness, frustration, anger and/or resentment. Disappointment is a natural part of life, so you will benefit from accepting that things may not always go as planned. Learning healthy ways to cope with disappointment is key to preventing it from becoming a major setback.

Have you ever felt disappointed? How did you overcome or handle it?

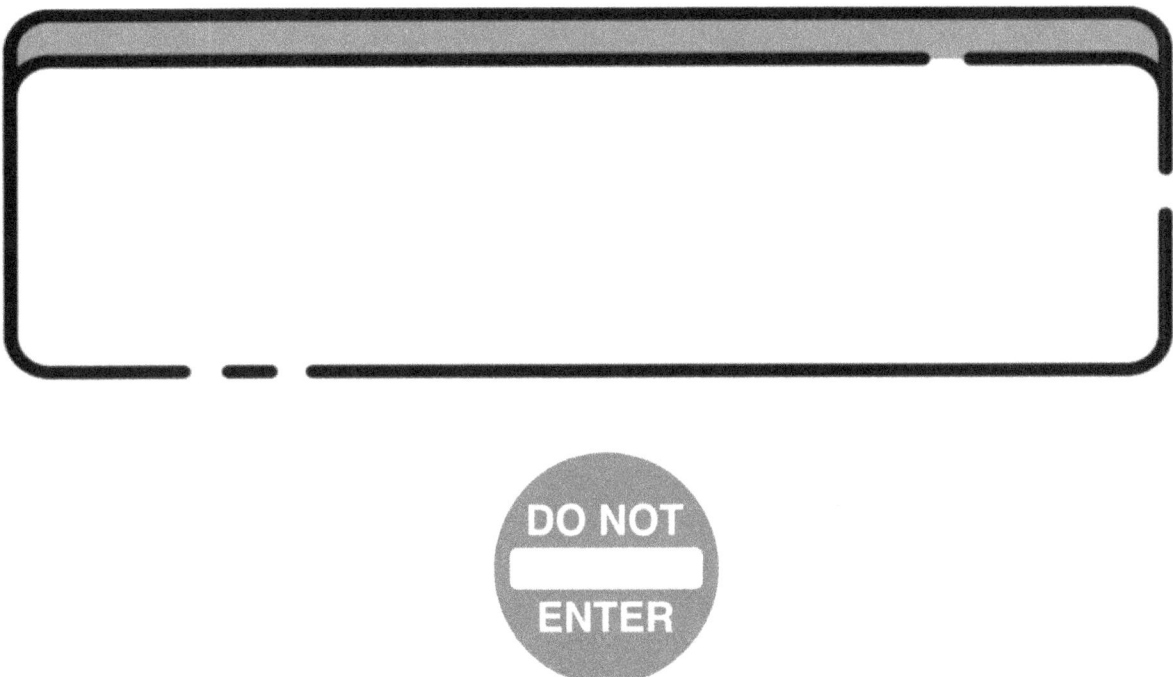

Disappointment happens in life, but you can use it to grow and learn. Focus on positive things in life, especially things you are grateful for each day.

Embarrassed

Embarrassment is when a person feels ashamed, shy, or uncomfortable. It usually happens when unwanted attention happens in a negative way. Falling in public, spilling food, or being laughed at are examples of embarrassment. If this happens, try to use humor and laugh at yourself, own the mistake (if this happens), and move on.

Have you ever felt embarrassed? If you feel comfortable, explain what happened.

Embarrassment is usually short-lived, and it happens to everyone. If it happens to you,

- remember to own it.
- apologize if necessary.
- laugh at yourself, if appropriate.
- move on, and let it go.

Fear

Fear is an emotion that happens when a person is in danger or feels threatened. Fear can happen as a result of a threat, such as seeing a dangerous animal or the thought of public speaking. When a person is afraid or fear something, he/she might start breathing heavily or sweating. The person may also feel his/her muscles tense up or feel sick in the stomach. Fear is natural, but when it is too much, it could lead to anxiety, paranoia and/or panic attacks. To deal with fear, it is best to practice slow, deep breathing to help the body calm down.

Have you ever felt fear? Explain what happened.

Fear can be dealt with in healthy ways. Make sure you take slow, deep breaths and practice self-talk. Say things like, "What's the worst that could happen?" or "I can handle this."

Grief

Grief can be one of the most difficult experiences in life. People go through stages when they are grieving a loss, such as the death of a loved one, a breakup, or perhaps the loss of a job. Every person does not go through every stage listed below, and some go through them in a different order.

Denial is usually the initial reaction to the loss where a person has a hard time accepting the situation. A person may feel disbelief, confusion, or avoidance. A person may feel shock and disbelief to the news of a loss.

Anger is usually when the reality sets in and the person is really upset. The person may be upset at him/herself or others. It is not uncommon for someone to experience feelings of anger and many emotions and thoughts can be difficult to process.

Bargaining is when a person may try to make a deal with him/herself or a higher power. For example, a person may make a promise to do better in exchange for something else.

Depression is when a person may have strong feelings of sadness and hopelessness. An individual may struggle without the person or thing he/she lost.

Acceptance is usually the final stage where the person comes to term with the reality of the loss. The grieving individual begins to find a way to move forward and continue living, even with the pain of the loss.

Have you ever experienced grief? Explain what happened. How did you get past it, or how will you?

Grief affects everyone in different ways, and there is no right way, wrong way, or time limit for recovery. Unfortunately, grief never completely disappears. There will be good and bad days, but a person can heal and rebuild a fulfilling life.

Guilt

Guilt is an emotion that people have in response to an action they have taken, a thought they had, or a feeling they experienced. Feelings of guilt happen after one has done something he/she should not have done. Cheating on a test or taking something without permission are two examples of when a person may feel guilty. If you feel guilty about something, admit that you feel that way and ask yourself why. Be kind to yourself, forgive yourself, and do better in the future.

Have you ever felt guilty about something? What happened?

Tips on Guilt

- Acknowledge your guilt.
- Ask for forgiveness, if necessary.
- Accept responsibility.
- Learn from mistakes.
- Be kind to yourself.
- Forgive yourself.

Irritated

Irritation is when you feel annoyed, frustrated, or impatient in a situation or with a person that is unpleasant. Normally, irritation is less intense than anger. All kinds of things can make a person feel irritated, such as disagreements, loud noises, or even exhaustion. To cope with irritation, a person should practice deep breathing and mindfulness. In addition, try to communicate calmly and explain what is bothering you without escalating the situation.

Have you ever felt irritated? How did you overcome the feelings?

To deal with irritation, practice the following:

- Identify the source of the irritation. Is it a person or a situation?
- Take a deep breath. Inhale through your nose and exhale through your mouth to stay calm.
- Pause before reacting, so you don't say anything you may regret.
- Practice self-talk and say to yourself, "I can handle and get through this."

Jealous

Jealousy is an emotion that happens when someone feels a threat to a valued relationship or something of importance. When one is jealous, feelings of insecurity, fear, or resentment, or envy may occur. Jealousy usually happens when an individual fears losing something important to him/her, such as attention, affection, or loyalty of a friend or family member to someone else. Jealousy can also develop in competitive situations where someone feels envious of another person's success. It is important to avoid comparing yourself to someone else, which could lead to jealousy. Focus on personal growth and building confidence in your strengths and accomplishments.

Have you ever felt jealous of someone? Why, and how did you feel?

- Use jealousy as an opportunity for self-reflection and growth.
- Acknowledge your feelings, so it doesn't lead to resentment.
- Do not compare yourself with others because you are unique.
- Remember, someone else's success doesn't take away from your potential.

Lonely

Loneliness is a deep emotional experience that happens when someone feels isolated and disconnected. Loneliness is linked to feelings of sadness, emptiness, or alienation. Loneliness is not the same as being alone, people can feel lonely when they don't have an emotional connection with those around them. Social loneliness is when someone does not have feelings of a sense of belonging or being part of a social group or community. Some common symptoms of loneliness include sadness, hopelessness, and emptiness. To help overcome loneliness, it could be good to initiate contact with friends and family. Being around others with similar interests can provide a sense of belonging.

Have you ever felt lonely? Why?

If you feel lonely, you can reach out to family and friends. Try to do things that bring you joy like reading, drawing, or writing. Remember to focus on positive things instead of dwelling on negative emotions.

Pressured

You should never feel intimidated or feel pressured to do something you do not want to do. You can respond in different ways, such as: *"No thanks. I am not interested. I don't do that; I need to stay focused on my goals. I've seen how being mean can hurt people, and I do not want to go down that path."* You should feel confident and know that it's okay to walk away from situations that make you uncomfortable.

Negative things can take away your energy, focus and motivation. It's better to focus on positive things and engage in some of your hobbies. Try to hang around people who bring you peace and joy.

How would you handle a situation in which you felt pressured to do something you did not feel comfortable doing?

Choose friends who respect and support your values. Peer pressure is less likely when you surround yourself with people who encourage positive behavior and make healthy choices.

Sadness

Sadness is an emotion when a person feels unhappiness, sorrow, or disappointment. It is usually caused by a loss, failure, or unfortunate event. Feelings of sadness is usually temporary, and it can be painful. However, sadness can serve as an important purpose, which allows individuals to process challenging experiences, reflect, and eventually heal. Sadness is a normal part of life and usually goes away over time. The death of a loved one or a pet, or the end of a friendship can cause sadness. Seeing a friend go through a difficult time can cause sadness as well, which shows empathy and compassion. It's okay to feel sad, and it's okay to show your emotions. Talk to a friend, family member, teacher or counselor, if you feel the need.

Have you ever felt sad? What makes you feel sad?

- Remember that healing from sadness takes time, so don't rush the process.
- Talk to someone you trust because sometimes, expressing your feelings can make you feel less alone.
- Engage in hobbies or activities to improve your mood.
- Practice deep breathing to help calm your mind when sadness feels overwhelming.
- Journaling may provide clarity to help reduce the feelings of sadness.

Scared

Feeling scared is a natural human emotion that happens in response to a perceived threat or danger. Feeling afraid or scared is important to survival, which helps a person avoid or react to dangerous situations. People feel scared for various reasons, including uncertainty, physical threats, and social fears. Some people feel scared when they are faced with real, immediate dangers that threaten their physical well-being. For example, encountering a wild animal or being in a natural disaster can make a person feel scared or afraid. Sometimes, a person may feel scared when he/she doesn't know what might happen in certain situations. Also, a person may fear failure, such as failing an exam. Again, when a person is scared, he/she may have a fast-beating heart, rapid breathing, tense muscles, sweating and/or an upset stomach.

Does anything make you feel scared or frightened?

Tips on Feeling Scared

- Acknowledge your fear and say to yourself, "It's okay to feel scared, and this is my body and mind trying to protect me."
- Practice self-talk and ask yourself, "What evidence do I have that this fear will come true?"
- Use visualization to picture yourself in control and handling any situation.
- Stay in the moment to avoid dwelling on the past and worrying about the future.

Stressed

Stress is when an individual is feeling worried or having mental tension caused by a difficult situation. Stress can be a positive or a negative experience, which leads to physical, emotional, and psychological reactions. Some stress is normal and can be helpful in a motivational way. However, prolonged or excessive stress can have negative effects on health and well-being. Like anxiety, when a person feels stressed, he/she may have a fast heartbeat, shortness of breath, tight muscles, and feel irritable. Stress can also give you headaches, tiredness, and an upset stomach.

Have you ever felt stressed? If yes, what made you feel stressed?

- To cope or deal with stress, you should stay in the moment and not worry about the past or future.
- Talk about what is bothering you or write it down.
- Breathe deeply by inhaling and exhaling.
- Exercise, even if it's just for a short walk.
- Do fun activities and hobbies, such as drawing, reading, or painting.
- Journal to stay calm and feel relaxed.
- Think about the things you appreciate in life.

Worried

Feeling worried is a mental process when a person focuses on potential problems or negative outcomes, which can lead to feelings of anxiety, uneasiness, and simply feeling afraid. Worrying involves repeated negative thoughts about future events or situations. Too much worrying can lead to stress and mental tiredness. It can be a big problem if the worrying is constant, especially if it interferes with daily life and well-being.

It's normal to worry and have concerns about such things as an upcoming test. Worrying becomes a problem when it occurs over long periods of time. Overthinking can happen as well. For example, a person may replay a conversation over and over, worrying about how someone interpreted a comment or worrying about every detail of a situation.

Have you ever felt worried? What makes you feel worried?

- Focus on a positive outcome, instead of focusing on a worst-case scenario.
- Take action by focusing on finding a solution to a problem.
- Again, practice deep breathing to stay calm and in the moment.
- Create a plan by writing down your worries and develop a plan on how to tackle them.

Worrying and Triggers

Understand triggers and how to deal with them prior to them happening is a benefit. There is a chart on the next page you can use to plan ahead for success.

A trigger is a person, place, thing, or situation that elicits an intense or unexpected emotional response or causes an individual to relive a past trauma.

How does it feel to be triggered?

While triggered, people may panic, feel overwhelmed, cry, act out, withdraw, or react defensively.

Some other symptoms when triggered may include feeling anxious, scared, or unsafe. A person may feel he/she has no control over his/her emotions, and he/she may experience increased heartbeat, difficulty breathing, and sweating.

If you ever experience feeling triggered, it is best to try and stay calm, breathe and if possible, take a break. Always try to think ahead of your response to a situation to avoid overreacting or saying something you may regret. Take time to listen to your feelings without judging yourself for feeling that way. Allow yourself to feel whatever emotion you're experiencing without trying to suppress it.

Having a grounding routine can help bring your focus back to the moment. Sharing your feelings with others and receiving empathy can be helpful in processing and coping with emotional triggers.

Tracking the Triggers

Can you name some things that trigger or worry you? List them below and think of a game plan to tackle these thoughts, triggers, and worries.

Triggers	Thoughts/Worries	Game Plan
Example: I have to take a test.	*I will do poorly on the test.*	*Study, and say, "I am going to do great!"*

Final Thoughts on Section 1

Are you having a hard time managing any emotions or feelings?

How are you currently handling these emotions or feelings?

Do you feel you are handling your feelings in the right way?

How can you improve?

Can you set some goals or a game plan to keep succeeding well in this area?

Remember to seek help if you need to and remember, YOU GOT THIS!

SECTION 2

Try to memorize some of these affirmations, or write a list of some, and keep them handy.

I deserve good things.
I am strong and powerful.
I am in control of my emotions.
I create my own happiness.
I can handle difficult things.
I will always try my best.
I will be kind to myself and others.
I will learn from my mistakes, grow, and help others.
I will achieve greatness.

Can you create some of your own affirmations?

The Alphabet

Recite the alphabet backwards in your head!

Now write it here:

1.
2.
3.
4.
5.
6.
7.
8.
9.
10.
11.
12.
13.
14.
15.
16.
17.
18.
19.
20.
21.
22.
23.
24.
25.
26.

This is a technique to use to distract yourself from perhaps an unpleasant situation. You can do this as often as necessary to stay calm, cool, and collected.

Blowing Bubbles to Stay Calm

Pretend you are blowing bubbles
Breathe in
Breathe out, pretend to blow lots of bubbles
What color are the bubbles?
Are the bubbles pink?
Are the bubbles blue?
Are the bubbles clear?
Again, pretend to blow bubbles
Breathe in
Breathe out, pretend to blow lots of bubbles
What color are the bubbles?
Do the bubbles smell like bubble gum?
Do the bubbles smell like spinach?
Do the bubbles smell like lemon tea?
How many bubbles can you pretend to see?

Breathing Exercise 1

Step 1

Take a deep breath
Breathe in
Breathe out
Repeat five times
Be mindful of what you are doing

Stay in the present moment
Relax and think positive thoughts

Take a deep breath
Breathe in
Breathe out

Repeat five times

Step 2

Do a fake, quiet yawn!
This may make you really want to yawn, which is okay.
Hopefully, the yawn interrupts any negative thoughts or feelings
Breathe in and breathe out.
Quietly say, "I feel so relaxed. I feel so at ease."

Repeat as many times as needed to really relax
and feel great about yourself.

Breathing Exercises 2

Sit in a chair with bent knees and relaxed shoulders.
Place your hand on your belly.
Breathe in slowly through your nose.
You should feel your belly moving under your hand.
As you exhale, tighten your muscles.
You should feel your belly fall inward.
Breathe out through your mouth with your lips.
Now, put more emphasis on the exhale than the inhale.
Keep exhaling for longer than usual before you slowly inhale again.
Repeat for five minutes if time allows or until you feel calm.

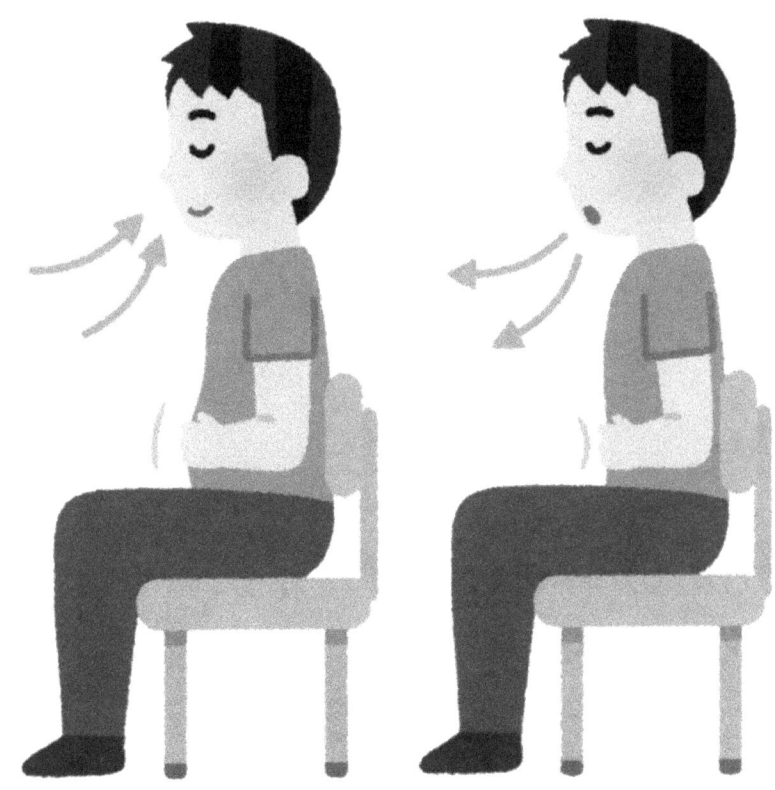

Coloring and drawing can be very relaxing. Give it a try.

Coloring Your Way to Calmness

Countdown by 5

Whenever you feel anxious or stressed, you can count down by 5 to feel calm.

100   95
        90   85
                80   75
                        70   65
                                    60
                                50   55
                            40   45
                        35
                    30
                25
            20
        15
        10
    5
0

Counting Backwards

Whenever you feel anxious or stressed, you can count backwards to feel calm.

Counting backwards

100

99 98 97 96 95 94 93 92 91 90
89 88 87 86 85 84 83 82 81 80
79 78 77 76 75 74 73 72 71 70
69 68 67 66 65 64 63 62 61 60
59 58 57 56 55 54 53 52 51 50
49 48 47 46 45 44 43 42 41 40
39 38 37 36 35 34 33 32 31 30
29 28 27 26 25 24 23 22 21 20
19 18 17 16 15 14 13 12 11 10
9 8 7 6 5 4 3 2 1 0

Create a Poem, Song, or Rap

Create a Story

Being creative may also help you feel calm. Create a story which can be funny, dramatic, scary, or whatever you like. Remember to include characters, a setting, a plot, climax, and resolution.

Create a Story Using the Five Senses
(Sight, Smell, Hearing, Taste, Touch)

You are going to create a story, but this time you will include your five senses.

Here is an example:
One day, I was watching television, and all of a sudden, I heard a loud noise. I ran in the kitchen and discovered my sister had burned the popcorn. It was all over the stove, and as I picked it up, it was slippery from the butter. I ate some, and it tasted yucky.

Creative Thinking

Feel free to draw a picture using your imagination and creativity. You can draw an animal, a funny clown, or anything you like.

In your own words, explain why you chose to draw that picture and what it means to you.

_____

_____

_____

DAILY GRATITUDE

/ /

TODAY I'M FEELING

POSITIVE AFFIRMATIONS

TODAY I'M GRATEFUL FOR

1.
2.
3.

SOMETHING I'M PROUD OF

MORE OF THIS:	LESS OF THIS:

I AM LOOKING FORWARD TO

Daily REFLECTION

Today is:

How I feel about today:

😞 😐 🙂 😊 😃

My act of kindness:

Reason for my rating

Something new I learned today:

Exercise Time

Here are some exercise ideas to make you feel less stress and more energetic!

Jumping jacks	Walking in place
Do a fun, crazy dance	Reach for the sky

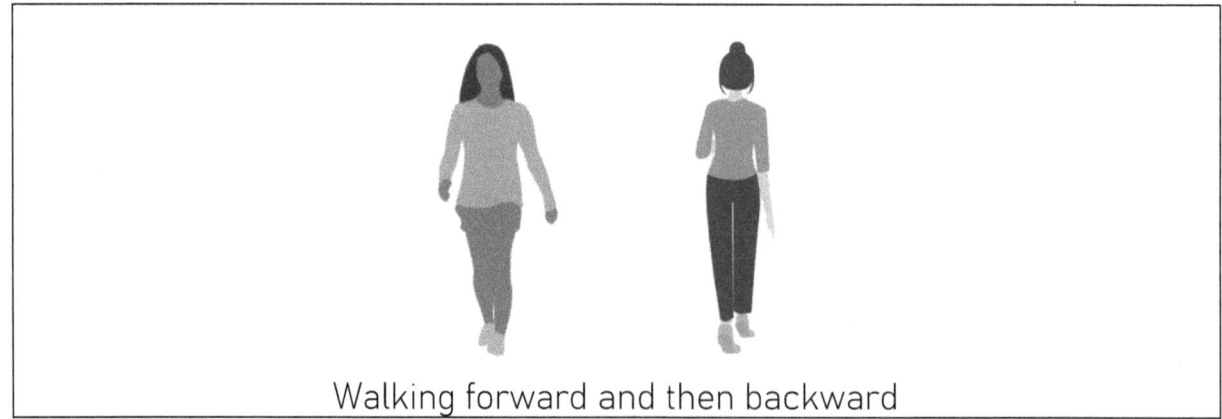

Walking forward and then backward

Grounding Techniques

Grounding Techniques are a way to bring your focus back to the present moment. These techniques can be used to keep you calm and help you with anxiety or a stressful situation. You can do some of the following:

Play the alphabet game, where you name something for each letter of the alphabet. For example: A is for Awesome, B is for Brave, and so forth.

Practice your breathing exercises to help you stay in the moment.

Focus on your five senses. Imagine being somewhere and take note of what you see, feel, hear, smell, or perhaps taste.

See	5 – What do you see? Look around you and take note of five things you see.
Feel	4 – Name four things you can feel and take note of the different textures.
Hear	3 – Listen for three sounds you hear, such as birds chirping or the sound of an air conditioner.
Smell	2 – Can you smell anything that is near you? If not, imagine some of your favorite scents, such as pumpkin pie or peppermint.
Taste	1 – Can you taste something right now? If not, imagine some things you like to eat.

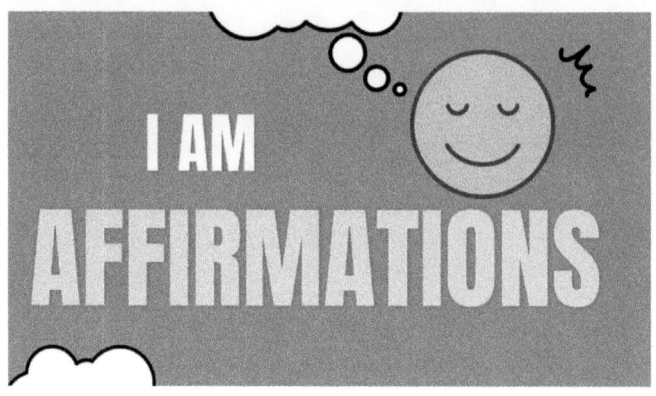

Directions: Read the phrase and then re-write the phrase in the box next to it. Read the phrase and decide if you like it and will say it as needed for an uplift.

I am amazing	
I am brave	
I am courageous	
I am dynamic	
I am energetic	
I am fabulous	
I am great	
I am happy	
I am intelligent	
I am joyful	
I am knowledgeable	
I am lively	
I am magnificent	
I am noble	
I am optimistic	
I am phenomenal	
I am qualified	
I am remarkable	
I am spectacular	
I am terrific	
I am unique	
I am victorious	
I am worthy	
I am xenial	
I am youthful	
I am zealous	

Journal Activity

Write about a tough day you had. What made it tough, and how did you react? Looking back at that day, would you react the same way or react in a different way?

Write about anything you want!

Name: _____ Date: _____

JOURNAL WRITING

Mental Health Check

MENTAL HEALTH CHECK IN

DATE: _____

HOW ARE YOU FEELING TODAY?
_____
_____
_____

WHAT DO YOU FEEL GOOD ABOUT?
_____
_____
_____

LIST ANY THINGS THAT BOTHER YOU:
_____
_____
_____

LIST THINGS YOU CAN DO TO IMPROVE YOUR HAPPINESS:
- ✓ _____
- ✓ _____
- ✓ _____

RANKING OF MY MENTAL HEALTH: ★ ★ ★ ★ ★

Mental health check in

DATE _____

HOW ARE YOU FEELING TODAY?
_____

HOW ARE YOU FEELING TODAY?

HOW CAN YOU IMPROVE YOUR MENTAL HEALTH?
_____

WHAT HAVE BEEN YOUR THREE DOMINANT EMOTIONS THIS WEEK?
○ _____
○ _____
○ _____

WHAT DO YOU FEEL GOOD ABOUT RIGHT NOW?
_____

THINGS THAT TRIGGERS NEGATIVE EMOTIONS
○ _____
○ _____
○ _____
○ _____

MY RANKING OF MY MENTAL HEALTH THIS WEEK
☆ ☆ ☆ ☆ ☆

Mindfulness

Mindfulness is the practice of being fully present and aware in the current moment. You are paying attention to your thoughts, feelings, and surroundings.

Mindfulness means being in the moment. You may be concentrating on your breathing, your heartbeat, or maybe the sounds around you.

Mindfulness is very important because it helps you control yourself and not become overwhelmed with emotions.

Mindfulness will help you make good decisions for yourself.

Think Positive

Positive Word List

Amazing Awesome Appreciative
Brilliant Brave Blissful
Cheerful Creative Conqueror
Dynamic Divine Delightful
Energetic Exuberant Enthusiastic
Fantastic Fine Fabulous Flourishing
Generous Grateful Genuine Gracious
Happy Healthy Hopeful Harmonious
Intelligent Imaginative Invigorated
Joyful Jubilant Jovial
Kind Keen Knowledgeable
Leader Likeable Luminous
Magnificent Marvelous Motivated
Nice Noble Nurturing
Outstanding Optimistic
Positive Peaceful Powerful Phenomenal
Qualified Quintessential
Resilient Remarkable Renewed
Special Spectacular Steadfast Successful Sensational
Terrific Thankful Trustworthy
Unique Understanding
Vibrant Valued Victorious Vibrant
Wonderful Wise Warmhearted
Xenial X-Factor
Youthful Yearn
Zany Zealous

Puzzles and games can help you relax. Can you find all the words in the list?

Relaxation

S	I	T	V	E	L	I	C	I	I	U	S	B	U
E	O	E	I	L	D	E	R	A	U	V	T	L	A
F	I	E	S	P	B	D	L	T	R	A	E	I	S
X	T	D	U	E	C	R	U	L	L	E	E	N	S
A	C	L	A	U	E	O	E	L	I	M	S	U	E
E	A	A	L	N	P	C	E	A	H	H	L	K	N
R	L	X	I	I	L	Y	S	I	T	P	C	I	L
U	M	A	Z	U	C	E	A	R	U	H	E	N	U
T	N	R	A	I	R	C	R	F	U	I	E	D	F
A	E	E	T	U	S	E	H	A	P	P	Y	N	D
N	S	L	I	G	R	A	T	I	T	U	D	E	N
C	S	A	O	E	V	I	T	I	S	O	P	S	I
N	N	X	N	T	S	E	R	A	F	S	B	S	M
T	T	A	E	C	L	P	E	A	C	E	F	U	L

SMILE
VISUALIZATION
REST
BREATHE
CARE
PEACEFUL
HAPPY
KINDNESS
MINDFULNESS
RELAX
CALMNESS
NATURE
CHILL
POSITIVE
GRATITUDE

The answers are in the back of the workbook.

Things I Like

Think of everything or everyone you care about and write nice things about the person or the things you like:

Trace the Patterns While Taking a Deep Breath

Trace the Patterns While Taking Deep Breaths (Part 2)

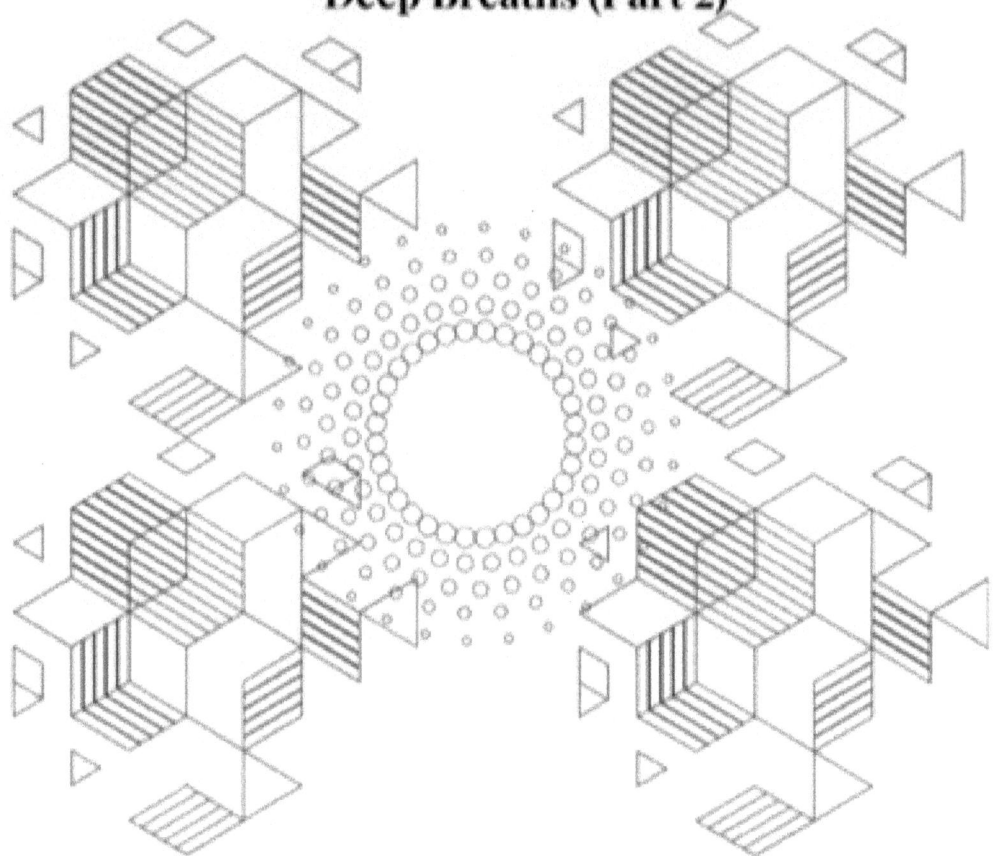

Visualization

Visualization is a picture you make in your mind. Imagine sitting near a waterfall or on the sand on a beach. Notice what sounds you hear as the water gently flows. If any negative thoughts pop into your head, you can watch the thoughts flow away. The more you do this, the calmer you will feel. Do you have any thoughts you want to flow away?

More About Feelings

Record your feelings to determine if certain things or time of the day make you feel a certain way. Understanding how you feel can help you manage your emotions and behavior. You can work through these thoughts and emotions using some of the coping skills you learned.

When I feel anger, I will:
When I feel sad, I will:
When I feel stressed, I will:
When I feel irritated, I will:
When I feel anxious, I will:
When I feel embarrassed, I will:
When I feel frustrated, I will:
When I feel pressured, I will:

Always remember
Life will be challenging
You can and will get through things
Don't ever hurt yourself
Don't ever hurt others
Don't destroy property

You Got This!

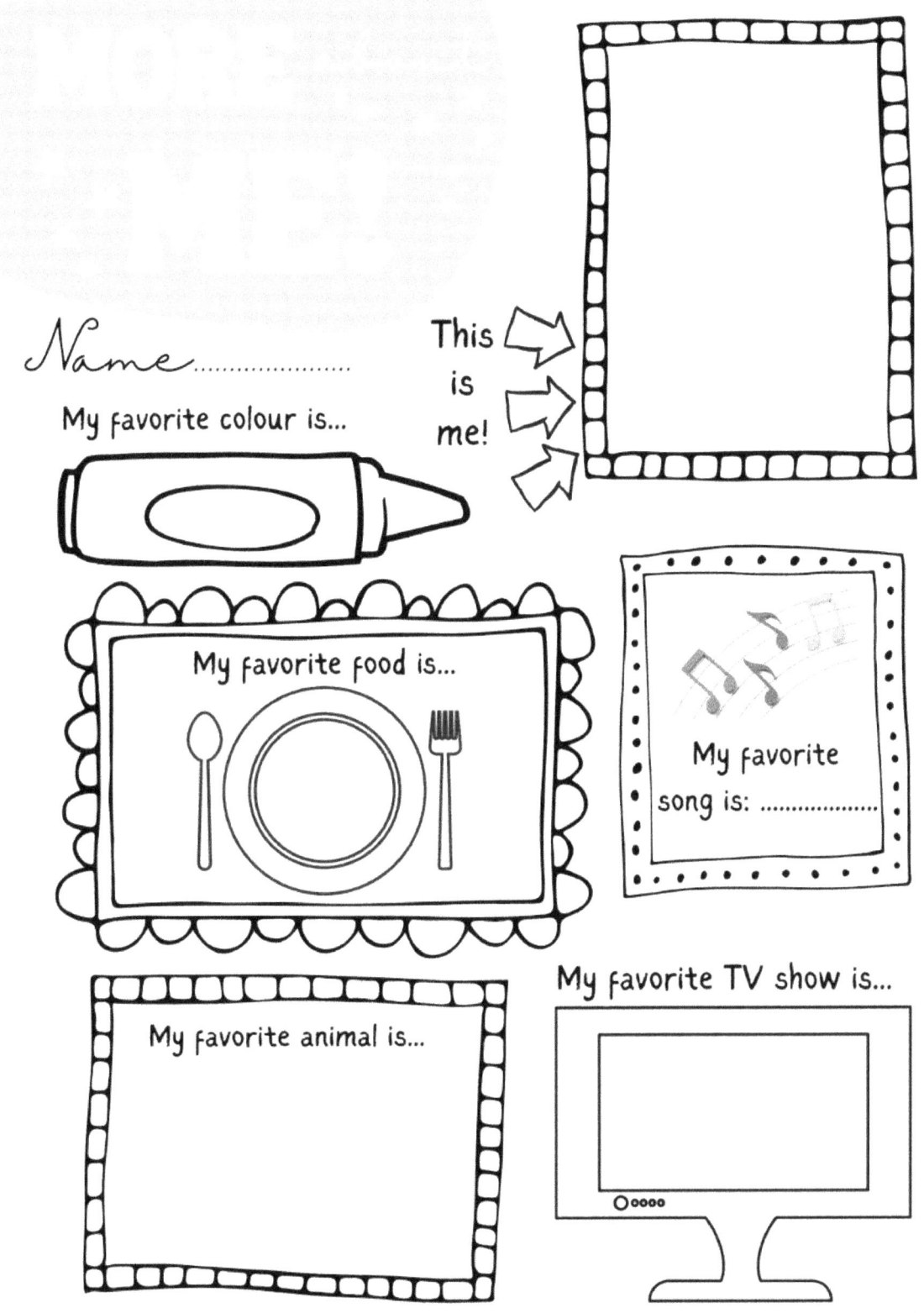

SECTION 3

Character

Character refers to your moral, ethical, and mental qualities that define how you think, behave, and interact with others. Character reflects a person's integrity, honesty, and moral strength, and it is often judged by how you respond in difficult situations. Character is not what you do when others are watching, but it is what you do when no one is looking.

Honesty, kindness, integrity, responsibility, courage, and respect builds character. Also, integrity refers to having a strong sense of right and wrong, and you should always strive to do the right thing. Character is necessary for personal development, relationships, and society as a whole.

What are the qualities that give a person a great character?

Keep in mind that developing a strong character takes effort and commitment.

Confidence

Confidence is the belief in one's abilities, qualities, and judgement. Positive self-talk has a big impact on your confidence. Focusing on what you do well can boost your confidence and self-worth. Confidence in your abilities can lead to higher motivation and a strong desire to succeed. Having confidence helps a person make good decisions, accomplish tasks, learn from mistakes, and continue growing. When problems arise, a person with great confidence in him/herself will have the ability to be resilient.

Name some things a person should say to him/herself to build confidence.

Discovering Differences

Discovering and embracing differences involves having an open mind, understanding, and empathy. It's important to appreciate and learn the unique qualities, backgrounds, and perspectives of other people. Doing this enriches personal growth, relationships, and builds community. To do this, ask questions to gain understanding and be an active listener.

Name a person you know and list the similarities and differences you two have:

We live in a diverse world, and a great way to get to know others is to learn about their traditions and values. Knowledge is powerful, and as you learn more and more, you develop a deeper understanding of the world.

Emotional Regulation

Emotional Regulation is the ability to manage and respond to emotional experiences in a balanced way. Being able to manage your emotions will help you respond thoughtfully, rather than react impulsively. This is important because it helps you handle stress, maintain good relationships, and stay focused on your goals. You never want to act impulsively and have regret. When unexpected things happen, remember to breathe and practice mindfulness. You can also practice positive, calming self-talk to avoid feeling anxious or frustrated.

Name at least two things you can do that is positive or productive when you are upset, instead of reacting impulsively.

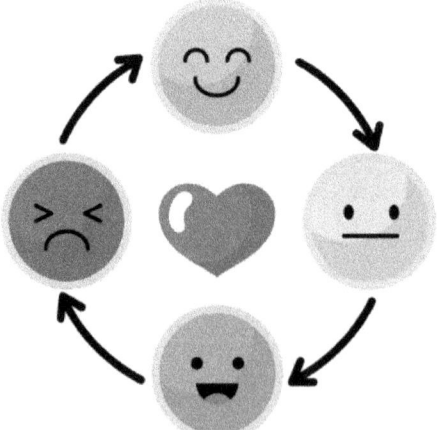

Another benefit of emotional regulation is that it helps with making good, thoughtful choices. Emotional regulation will help you feel empowered and resilient as you navigate through life.

Finding Joy

Finding joy each day involves appreciating the present moment, welcoming positive emotions, and finding purpose. Finding joy can come from fun activities you enjoy. Doing fun projects, learning new skills, and helping others could bring you joy. Finding joy in life could include positive affirmations, focusing on good things, and appreciating success. Peacefulness and finding joy may feel fulfilling and rewarding and may contribute towards your growth and accomplishment. Also, it is important to embrace imperfection, which allows you to find joy in your journey. Enjoy the process, and always celebrate what you have accomplished and the goals you have reached.

Name a few things that bring you joy:

Goal Setting

Setting goals is important because it gives you a clear sense of direction and keeps you focused on things that matter to you. Setting goals is also important for personal growth and a sense of purpose. Both short-term and long-term goals can create a roadmap for success. Setting goals can be very motivational and help you push through life's challenges. When you keep track of your progress, you can measure how far you have reached, determine what else you may need to do, and create new goals to help you continue to reach greatness. Goals can help you prioritize things and help you manage your time. Setting goals can also help you with self-discipline, build good habits, and keep you on track with your commitment.

Name at least 3 goals you have for yourself:

Gratitude

Gratitude is being thankful and appreciating the positive aspects of life. Gratitude is being thankful for what you have instead of focusing on what you don't have. A person can have gratitude for people or experiences, which can improve emotional well-being and help appreciate life. It's important to focus on the good things in your life, such as kind gestures from people and support from your family.

When you have gratitude, it strengthens your relationships and creates a deep connection. Also, gratitude is linked to happiness because it makes people feel good about what they have. Other benefits of gratitude may be less stress and better physical health. Some people write in their journal things they are grateful for each day, which can create a calming and reflective way to end your day.

Name all the things you are grateful for:

Happiness

Happiness is when you have feelings of joy, contentment, and satisfaction. Your mindset, relationships, and values can contribute to your happiness. Sometimes, happiness can come from short-term experiences, but true and lasting happiness often comes from a deep sense of meaning, purpose, and overall life satisfaction. Receiving good news, spending time with loved ones and achieving a personal goal, are examples of feeling happiness. People who practice gratitude and appreciation tend to feel happier because they focus on what they have, instead of what they do not have.

Name everything that makes you happy in the box below:

Learning new things, spending time with others, and focusing on positive things can contribute to happiness. Arts and crafts and creative projects can help you express your feelings and give structure to your day. Being creative can also give you a sense of positive accomplishment.

Identity

Identity is who you are, your beliefs, values, and experiences. A strong sense of identity helps you get through life, make good choices, and interact in meaningful ways with others. Identity is important because you know who you are and can feel confident in your actions and decisions. Another reason why identity is important is because it provides a foundation for you to build self-esteem and confidence. The more confident you are, the less likely you will give in to peer pressure and have feelings of uncertainty.

Who are you, and what makes you special?

Remember, having a sense of identity helps you make meaningful choices, encourages self-awareness, and provides the capability to remain resilient when dealing with difficult situations. Also, having a strong sense of identity encourages self-acceptance, so you can embrace your unique qualities, strengths and imperfections.

Kindness

Kindness involves being considerate, empathetic, and caring towards others. Kindness creates a more positive and supportive community, fostering mutual respect and cooperation. Kindness can be shown through small acts, such as smiling or saying hello to someone. Kindness is important for building trust, establishing relationships, and contributing to a supportive community. Showing acts of kindness can include helping someone, especially without being asked. Giving other people a compliment is another great way to show kindness. Another benefit of being kind is that it can boost happiness for both the giver and receiver.

Acts of Kindness

Can you think of an act of kindness you can show towards someone?

Here are 3 suggestions for you to show kindness:

Create something nice and give it to someone.	Write a 'thank you' note and give it to someone, such as a teacher or custodian.	With permission, give a toy or something you do not want any more to someone or to a charity.

Love Who I Am

Loving who you are is often referred to as self-love and self-acceptance. When you love yourself, you will have a fulfilling and happy life. Also, when you love and value yourself, you are able to have healthier relationships with others. You can set boundaries if necessary and form relationships based on mutual respect. Loving who you are will help you recognize how special you are, which helps build confidence. When you love yourself, you are able to make mistakes and learn and grow from them. You'll be less critical of yourself, which increases your self-acceptance. Lastly, loving who you are will allow you to treat yourself with kindness and understanding.

What do you love most about yourself?

Mental Health

Mental Health refers to a person's emotional, psychological, and social well-being. Your mental health influences how you think, feel, and behave each day. Good mental health is the ability to manage stress and bounce back from challenges. Signs of good mental health includes strong confidence, ability to manage responsibilities, and great coping skills.

Signs of poor mental health may include mood swings, sadness, irritability, and withdrawal from others. A few ways to promote good mental health includes physical exercise, good sleep, and relaxation. A great way to handle stress and have good mental health is to breathe deeply, meditate, and journal writing. If additional support is needed, it is a great idea to talk to a counselor.

What are some things you can do to make sure you have great mental health?

Mindset

Mindset refers to the set of beliefs, attitudes, and perceptions that shape how you view yourself and the world around you. There are two types of mindsets, and the first one is a fixed mindset, which is the belief that your abilities and intelligence are unchangeable. The other one is a growth mindset, which is the belief that your abilities can be developed and improved with effort and learning. A growth mindset is important because you will learn, grow, and improve over time. Your mindset determines how you handle problems and learn from mistakes. Another benefit of having a growth mindset promotes optimism and supports healthy coping skills.

Growth Mindset vs a Fixed Mindset

Growth Mindset	Fixed Mindset
Challenges are opportunities for growth.	I will not take a risk or challenge.
Feedback is helpful.	I do not like criticism.
Others' success is inspiring and pushes me to become better.	I feel threatened by others' success.
Failure is learning, and I will continue to do my best.	I will fail, and I will give up.

Try to have a positive, growth mindset instead of a negative one. What are some positive words you can use to accomplish this goal?

Positive Thinking and Positive Self-Talk

Positive Thinking is when you focus on the good parts of a situation, maintain an optimistic outlook, and remain hopeful, even when things may not look too good. Positive thinking is important because it can have a big impact on mental and physical health. Positive thinking can help you bounce back from challenges and can help you work through solutions. When you have positive thinking, you tend to have healthier relationships and will be less likely to experience feelings of anxiety and stress. Another benefit of positive thinking is it enhances motivation, which can lead to more success. When you think positively, you are more likely to set goals and take steps to accomplish those goals. Positive thinking increases your self-confidence and your overall sense of self-worth.

Turn negative talk into positive talk:

Instead of saying:	*Say this instead:*
"I'm not good at this."	"I will get better at this."
"I make so many mistakes."	"I will make mistakes as I learn things."
"I'll never understand this."	"I haven't gotten it yet."

Can you give an example of positive self-talk?

Purpose

A sense of purpose helps to have a clear understanding of what gives your life meaning. Knowing your sense of purpose helps you identify what's important to you and guides you on how to live your life. A sense of purpose helps you stay motivated with a desire to pursue your goals. When you have a sense of purpose, you are more likely to feel satisfied in life. Another benefit for knowing your purpose helps with maintaining happiness and resilience. Having and knowing your purpose may help you combat feelings of isolation and loneliness. Also, having a sense of purpose can help you feel connected to others in the world.

What is your sense of purpose in life?

Reflection

Reflection is when you think deeply about your actions, emotions, experiences, and thoughts to gain insight, understanding, and perspective. It allows you to learn from things that happened, and it helps with your personal growth. Reflection helps you with self-awareness where you can evaluate your strengths and weaknesses. When you reflect, it becomes easier to improve and work on items that did not have the best outcome. Reflection allows you to determine the pros and cons of different options you have and hopefully avoid impulsive behavior.

Think about your past few days and reflect on what went well and note anything that could have been better:

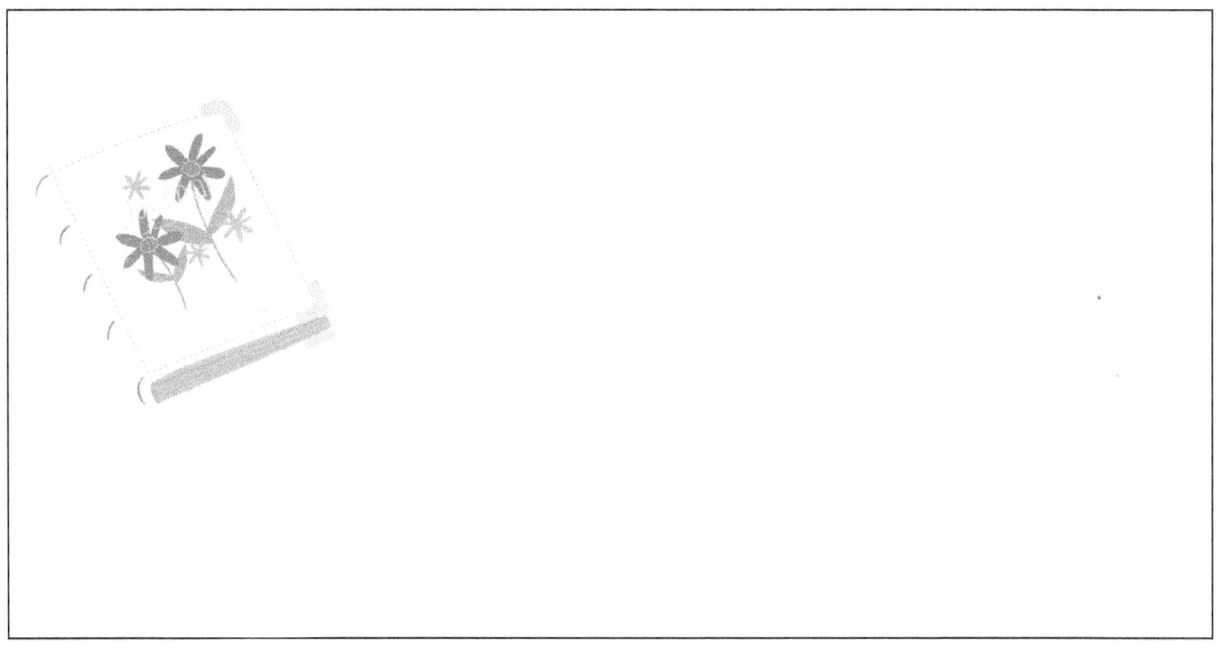

Another benefit of reflection is that it helps you to build emotional intelligence. Emotional intelligence helps you to have healthy relationships and deal with stress. Reflection encourages mindfulness and helps you gain insight about your experiences, feelings, and lessons learned.

Relationship Skills

Relationship Skills refer to the abilities and behaviors that help individuals build and maintain healthy, meaningful, and supportive relationships with others. To have great relationship skills, you will need to communicate effectively and resolve problems. Communication is key in expressing yourself, and it is important to listen to others. One of the benefits of great communication is to prevent misunderstandings, which helps with mutual respect. Throughout life, you will need skills to effectively communicate with others who have different backgrounds. Trust, respect, patience, and compromise are also key factors to have good relationship skills. As often as you can, try to have fun and be optimistic to make relationships more enjoyable.

Think of a friend you have. Name something special about him or her.

What would this same friend say about you?

What qualities do you look for in finding friends?

How would you positively deal with a situation if you found out someone said something about you that was not true?

What can you do to make sure you are being a good friend to someone?

Responsible Decision Making

Responsible Decision Making is the process of making thoughtful, informed, and ethical choices that show you care for your well-being and others. When you make responsible decisions, you look at different choices and decide what is probably best. Gathering as much information as possible, such as facts, opinions, and possible consequences can help make good decisions.

Reacting impulsively means you are responding too quickly and not giving much thought to your action. Responding in a careful, calm manner is good because you'll probably make a better choice.

Name a bad decision you made but learned from.

Can you recall a good decision you made?

Why do you make good choices?

Having responsible decision-making skills is crucial for personal success because of your informed decisions. Responsible decision making requires aligning your choices with your values and principles. Another benefit of responsible decision making is how it will affect others, such as family, friends, peers, and others. You will build trust with others and strengthen your sense of integrity.

Self-Awareness

Self-awareness is the ability to recognize and understand your own thoughts, emotions, behaviors, strengths, weaknesses, and motivations. Being self-aware of who you are helps you to know how to react in different situations and have insight to make good decisions. Another benefit of self-awareness is that it improves emotional intelligence, which helps you manage stress, handle conflicts, build confidence, and build better relationships.

Self-awareness allows you to react appropriately in different situations because of your emotional intelligence. Write the best decision in each scenario listed below:

If someone yells at you, you should:	If someone hits you, you should:
If someone lies on you, you should:	If you feel pressured to do something you do not want to do, you should:

Self-Esteem

Self-esteem refers to your sense of self-worth, value, and confidence in yourself. Self-esteem has a huge impact on how you feel about your identity, appreciate and care about yourself, and make good decisions. When you have high self-esteem, you have self-confidence and belief in your own abilities. Having a healthy self-esteem helps with your mental health, and it helps you manage stress. Also, you will be able to handle challenges, have a better mindset, and avoid negative self-talk. Having healthy self-esteem helps you interact effectively with others and helps you achieve your goals. As much as possible, try to surround yourself with people who are supportive and who uplift you, which will boost your confidence and self-worth.

The key component of self-esteem includes self-confidence, self-acceptance, self-respect, resilience, and knowing your sense of worth.

What can you do every day to build your self-esteem?

Self-Management

Self-Management is the ability to regulate your thoughts, emotions, and behaviors in a way that helps you achieve your goals. When you have self-management, you will take responsibility for your actions and emotions and have self-discipline. Self-discipline helps you stick to routines, meet deadlines, and focus on reaching your goals.

Self-management helps you stay calm, avoid overreacting, and stay in tune with emotional regulation. Another benefit of self-management is the ability to set goals, stay focused, and feel good about yourself. Self-management will help you with impulse control to avoid making decisions that could have a negative outcome. Self-management will help you with organization, which reduces chaos and helps you to focus on your goals and personal growth.

There are many benefits of self-management, such as reduction of stress, improved productivity, and impulse control. To develop self-management skills, you can:

- set clear goals
- create a routine
- reflect on your progress

Write down some goals and a routine to help with self-management.

Social Awareness

Social Awareness is the ability to understand and have empathy with other people's emotions and needs. When you have social awareness, you will understand people, groups, and be mindful of your actions and how they affect people around you. Empathy helps build relationships and helps you create a deeper connection. You will be able to respond with care, which should help with communication and avoid misunderstandings.

Social awareness will help you recognize facial expressions, tone of voice, and body language. Also, social awareness helps build strong relationships where there is respect and understanding, and hopefully trust.

Social awareness is important because it enhances your ability to understand how others feel or think, which builds mutual understanding and respect. Social awareness helps prevent misunderstandings, reduces conflict, and promotes trust.

Complete this statement. If I have social awareness, I will:

Teamwork

Teamwork is a group of individuals working together to achieve a common goal or complete a task. Effective teamwork includes cooperation, communication, and support using each other's strengths and abilities to accomplish things. The benefit of teamwork is the ability to achieve more, rather than working alone.

Sometimes, it can be difficult to work with other people, which is why it is important to have good communication and understanding to ensure team members can work together smoothly. When members of a team share the same goal, they may be more motivated to work their best to achieve success. It is important to establish clear goals, so everyone is working towards the same objective, and everyone should know their role and responsibility. Another benefit of teamwork is that a variety of different ideas and skills can spark creativity.

Have you ever been part of team? What are some great ways to make teamwork successful?

Time Management

Time Management is when you plan, organize, and control how you spend your time on different tasks and activities. Good time management is when you prioritize tasks, set goals, and make the best use of your time to meet deadlines and reduce procrastination. You will also meet deadlines and hopefully avoid stress. Avoiding procrastination is very important because you won't feel rushed, and you may have improved quality of work. A great way to improve time management is to create a "to do" list, prioritize each item, and check items off as you complete each one. You should feel good knowing how much you have done and feel accomplished.

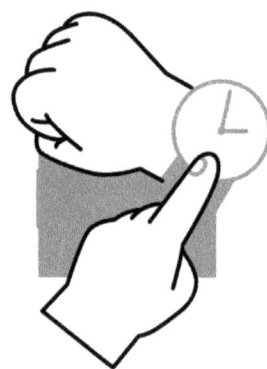

Good time management allows you to accomplish many things and feel productive. Time management allows you to think, plan, and make good decisions. To improve your time-management skills, creating lists may be helpful.

To Do List

SECTION 4

CONSTRUCTION ZONE

Wellness Toolkit

Add a few items from the list to your toolkit below that will help you stay calm, relax, and think before reacting. Keep this handy or try to memorize some of them.

Affirmations	Daily Gratitude
Alphabet	Exercise Time
Blowing Bubbles to Stay Calm	Grounding Techniques
Breathing Exercises	Journal Writing
Coloring Your Way to Calmness	Things I Like
Countdown and Counting Backwards	Mindfulness
Create a Poem, Song, or Rap	Trace the Patterns
Create a Story Using the 5 Senses	Visualization

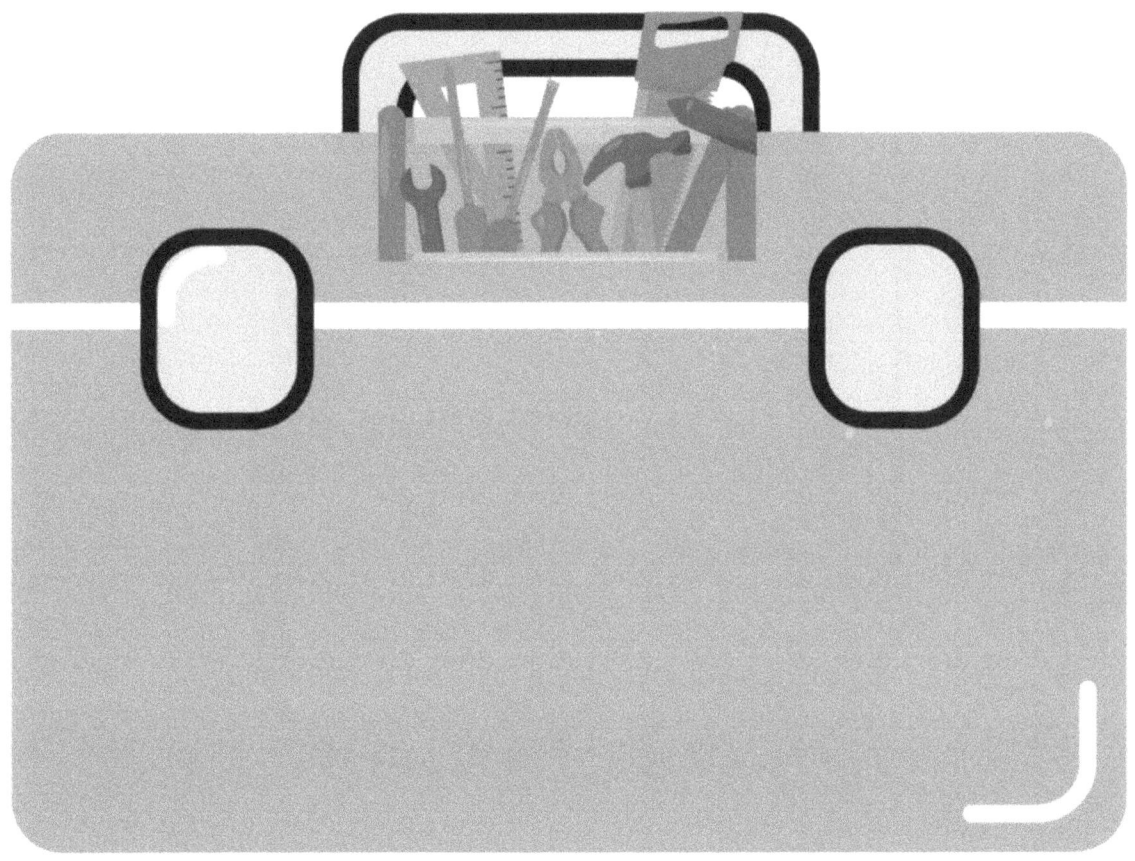

_____'s Self-Esteem Jar
Add Your Name

Make a list of your positive qualities, accomplishments, and things you like about yourself. Example: "I am a good friend." "I'm great at solving math problems." "I'm a good listener." "I try my best when things are hard."

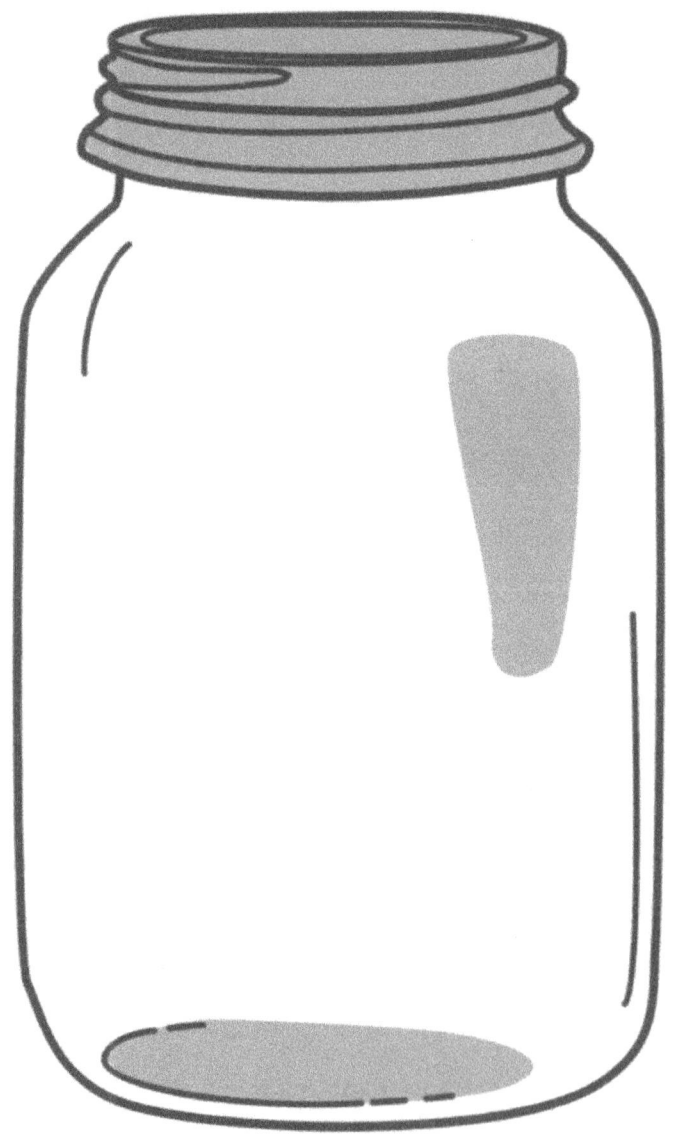

Confidence Collage

Confidence is believing in yourself and your abilities. In each square below, you can cut out pictures, words, or phrases from magazines that represent:
- Your strengths (e.g., images of sports, art, music).
- Your accomplishments (e.g., trophies, books, teamwork).
- Goals or aspirations (e.g., travel destinations, careers).
- Positive affirmations (e.g., "I can do it," "Be strong," "Keep trying").

You can add your own drawings or words if you can't find something in the magazines.

DATE: _____

ACTION PLAN

LIST YOUR GOALS HERE:
_____
_____
_____

WHAT MAKES YOU HAPPY:
_____
_____
_____

I WILL SUCCEED BY:
_____
_____
_____

I PLAN ON:
- ✓ _____
- ✓ _____
- ✓ _____
- ✓ _____

MY GOALS

I will:

I will:

Draw a Picture

Draw a picture of your newly constructed self. List all your great qualities (if you need help thinking of words, choose from the positive word list in the yellow section of this workbook).

What is your action plan to succeed in life?

What are some goals you have?

What is your game plan to truly get what you want in life?

Express Yourself

In a perfect world, I would see this:

When I experience emotions in the red zone, I will handle them by:

I will remember to breathe deeply and:

I will practice my self-talk by saying:

Do Something Fun

Write a letter to a friend.

Watch something funny or think of something funny.

Play cards or play a game.

Talk to a classmate or friend and try to get to know him/her better.

Write a poem.

Read a good book.

Listen to music to help you relax.

Write your own song and plan on singing it.

Do puzzles to take your mind away from stress.

Do a kind act to cheer someone up.

Celebrate Me

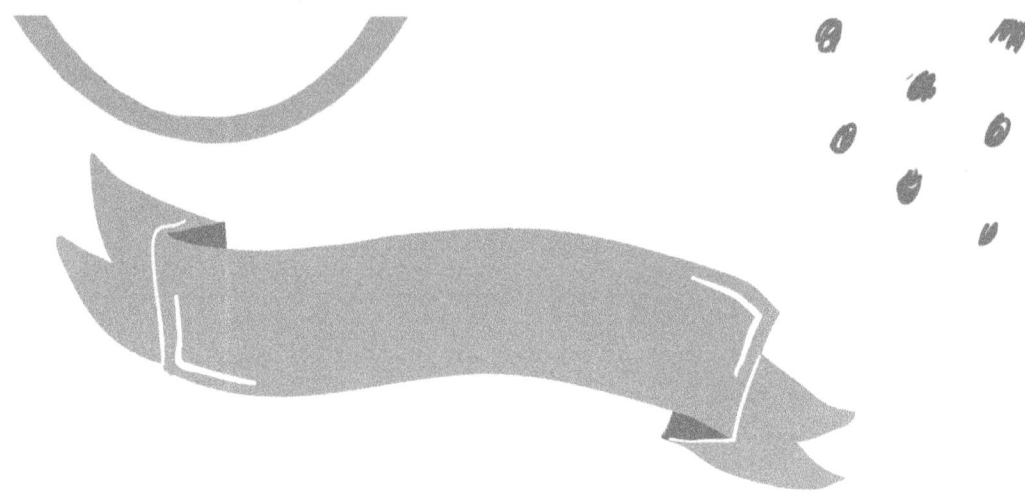

Give yourself a compliment:
_____

Celebrate something you have accomplished:
_____

What do you love about yourself?
_____

Notes

Answers to Word Search

S	I	T	V	E	L	I	C	I	I	U	S	B	U
E	O	E	I	L	D	E	R	A	U	V	T	L	A
F	I	E	S	P	B	D	L	T	R	A	E	I	S
X	T	D	U	E	C	R	U	L	L	E	E	N	S
A	C	L	A	U	E	O	E	L	I	M	S	U	E
E	A	A	L	N	P	C	E	A	H	H	L	K	N
R	L	X	I	I	L	Y	S	I	T	P	C	I	L
U	M	A	Z	U	C	E	A	R	U	H	E	N	U
T	N	R	A	I	R	C	R	F	U	I	E	D	F
A	E	E	T	U	S	E	H	A	P	P	Y	N	D
N	S	L	I	G	R	A	T	I	T	U	D	E	N
C	S	A	O	E	V	I	T	I	S	O	P	S	I
N	N	X	N	T	S	E	R	A	F	S	B	S	M
T	T	A	E	C	L	P	E	A	C	E	F	U	L

Final Project

Now that you've completed the workbook, feel free to create something showing what you have learned. You can choose one or more of the following. (Use the space on the next page for this activity).

- Poster
- Song
- Poem
- Letter
- Play or Skit
- Journal Activity
- Dance
- Coloring Book
- Pop-up Book
- Report
- Brochure
- Cartoon Strip
- Essay
- Speech
- Biography
- Short Story

Conclusion

Congratulations! You did it! I hope this resource provided valuable information to manage your feelings and emotions. Think about all you have learned and the importance of using the skills you've acquired. You have strategies to use during difficult times and in tough situations. You have the tools to stay calm, the ability to think before reacting, and the talent to think positively. Know that everything is going to be okay, and seek help if you need it.

Please continue to write in a journal about your journey through life, especially when things are bothering you and you need to get the bad thoughts out of your head. Remind yourself of things you are grateful for, exercise deep breathing, and always practice positive self-talk.

Best Wishes to You on Your Journey in Becoming an Adult

Bibliography

Bourque, K. (2024) *CBT Workbook for Kids*. Brisbane, Australia: Ricca's Garden.

Carter, JV. (2008) *The Blueprint for Greatness!* California: Inspiration 52.

Halloran, J. (2018) *Coping Skills for Kids Workbook*. Wisconsin: PESI Publishing and Media.

Lozier, C. (2018) *DBT Therapeutic Activity Ideas for Working with Teens*. London and Philadelphia: Jessica Kingsley Publishers.

McKay, M., Wood, J.C., & Brantley, J. (2007) *The Dialectical Behavior Therapy Skills Workbook*. California: New Harbinger Publications, Inc.

Sherman, H. (2020) *Mindfulness Workbook for Kids*. California: Rockridge Press.

White-Elliott, C. (2023) *Living Life Without a Mask Authentically & Unapologetically You.* California: CLF Publishing Collaborative, LLC.

Acknowledgements

I would like to express my sincere thanks and gratitude to:

First and foremost, God, who is everything to me, Webster, Jasmine, Son-in-Love, Vincent, my sisters, nieces, nephews, and family. To my amazing friends, church family, and the wonderful people I work with every day. A special thank you to Estela, who has guided me every step of the way on this project.

About the Author

Kim Roshone is an educator in Los Angeles, California. She received a Bachelor of Arts degree in Sociology, a Master of Education degree in School Counseling from California State University, Dominguez Hills, and a reading certificate from USC. For over 25 years, she has worked with students who are incarcerated and who have inspired her to create this resource. She is the creator of Red Yellow Green Feelings.com where additional resources can be found.

www.ingramcontent.com/pod-product-compliance
Lightning Source LLC
Chambersburg PA
CBHW061116170426
43198CB00026B/2993